The Pythagorean Philosophy

T. J. DeBoer

Kessinger Publishing's Rare Reprints

Thousands of Scarce and Hard-to-Find Books
on These and other Subjects!

- Americana
- Ancient Mysteries
- Animals
- Anthropology
- Architecture
- Arts
- Astrology
- Bibliographies
- Biographies & Memoirs
- Body, Mind & Spirit
- Business & Investing
- Children & Young Adult
- Collectibles
- Comparative Religions
- Crafts & Hobbies
- Earth Sciences
- Education
- Ephemera
- Fiction
- Folklore
- Geography
- Health & Diet
- History
- Hobbies & Leisure
- Humor
- Illustrated Books
- Language & Culture
- Law
- Life Sciences

- Literature
- Medicine & Pharmacy
- Metaphysical
- Music
- Mystery & Crime
- Mythology
- Natural History
- Outdoor & Nature
- Philosophy
- Poetry
- Political Science
- Science
- Psychiatry & Psychology
- Reference
- Religion & Spiritualism
- Rhetoric
- Sacred Books
- Science Fiction
- Science & Technology
- Self-Help
- Social Sciences
- Symbolism
- Theatre & Drama
- Theology
- Travel & Explorations
- War & Military
- Women
- Yoga
- *Plus Much More!*

We kindly invite you to view our catalog list at:
http://www.kessinger.net

III. THE PYTHAGOREAN PHILOSOPHY.

1. NATURAL PHILOSOPHY.

1. Euclid and Ptolemy, Hippocrates and Galen, some
portion of Aristotle, and, in addition, an abundant Neo-
Platonic Literature, — indicate the elements of Arabic Natural
Philosophy. It is a popular philosophy, which, chiefly through
the instrumentality of the Sabaeans of Harran, found accep-
tance with the Shi'ites and other sects, and which in due
course impressed not only court circles, but also a large
body of educated and half-educated people. Stray portions
of it were taken from the writings of the "Logician",
— Aristotle, — *e. g.* from the "Meteorology", from the
work "On the Universe", which has been attributed to
him, from the "Book of Animals", from the "Psychology",
and so on; but its general character was determined by
Pythagorean-Platonic teaching, by the Stoics, and by sub-
sequent astrologers and alchemists. Human curiosity and
piety were fain to read the secrets of the Deity in the
book of his Creation, and they proceeded in this search
far beyond practical requirements, which merely called for
a little arithmetic to serve in the division of inheritances
and in trade, and a little astronomy besides, to determine
the proper times for celebrating the functions of religion.

Men hastened to gather wisdom from every quarter, and in so doing they manifested a conviction, which Masudi accurately expressed, when he said: "Whatever is good should be recognized, whether it is found in friend or foe". Indeed Ali, the prince of believers, is reported to have said: "The wisdom of the world is the believer's strayed sheep: take it back, even though it come from the unbelieving".

Pythagoras is the presiding genius of Mathematical study in Islam. Greek and Indian elements are mingled in it, it is true, but everything is regarded from a Neo-Pythagorean point of view. Without studying such branches of Mathematics, as Arithmetic and Geometry, Astronomy and Music, no one, they said, becomes a philosopher or an educated physician. The Theory of Numbers, — prized more highly than Mensuration, because it appeals less to the outward vision, and should bring the mind nearer the essence of things, — gave occasion to the most extravagant puerilities. God is, of course, the great Unity, from whom everything proceeds, who himself is no number, but who is the First Cause of Number. But above all, the number Four, — the number of the elements and so on, — was held in high favour by the philosophers; and by-and-by nothing in heaven or earth was spoken of or written about, except in sentences of four clauses and in discourses under four heads.

The transition from Mathematics to Astronomy and Astrology was rapid and easy. The old Eastern methods, which came into their hands, continued to be applied even by the court-astrologers of the Omayyads, but with still greater thoroughness at the Abbasid court. In this way

they arrived at speculations which ran counter to the re-
vealed Faith, and which therefore could never be approved
of by the guardians of religion. The only antithesis which
existed for the Believer was — God and the World, or
this life and the next; but for the Astrologer there were
two worlds, one of the Heavens and another of the Earth,
while God and the life beyond were in the far distance.
According to the different conceptions entertained of the
relation which subsisted between the heavenly bodies and
sublunary things, either a rational Astronomy was developed, or a fantastic Astrology. Only a few kept entirely
free from Astrological delusions. As long, in fact, as the
science was dominated by the Ptolemaic system, it was
easier for the completely uneducated man to jeer at what
was absurd in it than it was for the learned investigator
to disprove the same. For the latter indeed this earth with
its forms of life was a product of the forces of the heavens,
a reflection of celestial light, an echo of the eternal harmony
of the Spheres. Those then who ascribed conception and
will to the Spirits of the stars and spheres, held them
as the representatives of Divine providence, and thus traced
to their agency both what is good and what is evil, seeking
also to foretell future events from the situation of their
orbs, by means of which they bring their influence to bear
upon earthly things in accordance with steadfast laws. Others,
it is true, had their doubts about this secondary providence,
on grounds of experience and reason, or from the Peripatetic
belief that the blessed existences of the heavens are Spirits
of pure intellect, exalted above conception and will, and
in consequence above all particularity that appeals to the
senses, so that their providential influence is directed only

to the good of the whole, but never can have reference to any individual occurrence.

3. In the domain of Natural Science Muslim learned men collected a rich body of material; but hardly in any case did they succeed in really treating it scientifically. In the separate Natural sciences, the development of which we cannot follow up in this place, they clung to traditional systems. To establish the wisdom of God and the operations of Nature, — which was regarded as a power or emanation of the World-Soul, — alchemistic experiments were instituted, the magical virtues of talismans tested, the effects of Music upon the emotions of men and animals investigated, and observations made on physiognomy, while attempts were also set on foot to explain the wonders of the life of sleep and of dreams, as well as those of soothsaying and prophecy, &c. As might be expected, the centre of interest was Man, as the Microcosm which must combine in itself all the elements and powers of the world together. The essential part of Man's being was held to be the Soul; and its relation to the World-Soul, and its future lot were made subjects of enquiry. There was also a good deal of speculation about the faculties of the soul and their localization in the heart and the brain. One or two adhered to Galen, but others went farther than he did, and made out five inner senses corresponding to the five outer ones, — a theory which, along with similar natural mysteries, was traced to Apollonius of Tyana.

Obviously the most diverse attitudes towards religious doctrine were possible in the study of Mathematical and Physical Science. But the propaedeutic sciences, as soon as they came forward on their own account, were always

dangerous to the Faith. The assumption of the eternity of
the world, and of an uncreated matter in motion from
all eternity, — was readily combined with Astronomy. And
if the movement of the Heavens is eternal, so too are, no
doubt, the changes which take place on earth. All the king-
doms of Nature then, according to many teachers, being
eternal, the race of man is eternal also, wheeling round
and round in an orbit of its own. There is therefore nothing
new in the world: the views and ideas of men repeat themselves like everything else. All that can possibly be done,
maintained or known, has already been and will again be.

Admirable discourse and lamentation were expended upon
this theme, without much advancing thereby the interests
of Science.

4. The science of Medicine, which on obvious grounds
was favoured by the ruling powers, appears to have proved
somewhat more useful. Its interests furnished one of the
reasons, and not the least considerable, which induced
the Caliphs to commission so many men to translate Greek
authors. It is therefore not to be wondered at that the
teachings of Mathematics and Natural Science, together with
Logic, also affected Medicine intimately. The old-fashioned
doctor was disposed to be satisfied with time-honoured
magical formulae, and other empirical expedients; but
modern society in the ninth century required philosophical
knowledge in the physician. He had to know the "natures"
of foods, stimulants or luxuries, and medicaments, the
humours of the body, and in every case the influence of
the stars. The physician was brother to the astrologer,
whose knowledge commanded his respect, because it had
a more exalted object than medical practice. He had to

attend the lectures of the alchemist, and to practise his art in accordance with the methods of Mathematics and Logic. It was not enough for the fanatics of education in the ninth century that a man had to speak, believe and behave in accordance with *Qiyas*, — that is to say, with logical correctness: he must, over and above, submit to be treated medically in accordance with *Qiyas*. The principles of Medicine were discussed in learned assemblies at the court of Wathik (842—847) like the foundations of Doctrine and Morals. The question, in fact, was asked, prompted by a work of Galen's, whether Medicine relies upon tradition, experience or rational knowledge, or whether on the other hand it derives its support from the principles of Mathematics and Natural Science by means of logical deduction (*Qiyas*).

5. The Natural Philosophy, which has just been rapidly sketched, actually stood for Philosophy with the most of the scholars of the ninth century, as contrasted with theological dialectic, and was styled Pythagorean. It lasted even into the tenth century, when its most important representative was the famous physician Razi († 923 or 932). Born in Rai he received a mathematical education and studied Medicine and Natural Philosophy with great diligence. He was averse to dialectic and was only acquainted with Logic as far as the categorical figures of the First Analytics. After having practised as director of the hospital in his native city and in Bagdad, he entered upon his travels and resided at various princely courts, amongst others at the court of the Samanid Mansur ibn Ishaq, to whom he dedicated a work on Medicine.

Razi has a high opinion of the medical profession and of the study which it demands. The wisdom of a thousand

years, contained in books, he prizes more than the experiences of the individual man gained in one short life, but
he prefers even these to deductions of the "Logicians" which
have not been tested by experience.

He thinks that the relation between the body and the
soul is determined by the soul. And seeing that in this
way the circumstances and sufferings of the soul admit of
being discerned by means of the physiognomy, the medical
man has to be at the same time a physician of the soul.
Therefore he drew up a system of spiritual medicine, —
a kind of Dietetic of the Soul. The precepts of Muslim
law, like the prohibition of wine, and so on, gave him no
concern, but his freethinking seems to have led him into
pessimism. In fact he found more evil than good in the
world, and described inclination as the absence of dis-
inclination.

High though the value was which Razi put upon Aristotle
and Galen, he did not give himself any special trouble to
gain a more profound comprehension of their works. He
was a devoted student of Alchemy, which in his view was
a true art, based on the existence of a primeval matter,
— an art indispensable to philosophers, and which, he
believed, had been practised by Pythagoras, Democritus,
Plato, Aristotle and Galen. In opposition to Peripatetic
teaching he assumed that the body contained in itself the
principle of movement, a thought which might certainly
have proved a fruitful one in Natural Science, if it had
been recognized and farther developed.

Razi's Metaphysic starts from old doctrines, which his
contemporaries ascribed to Anaxagoras, Empedocles, Mani
and others. At the apex of his system stand five co-eternal

principles, — the Creator, the Universal Soul, the First or Primeval matter, Absolute Space, and Absolute Time or Eternal Duration. In these the necessary conditions of the actually existing world are given. The individual sense-perceptions, generally, presuppose an existing Matter, just as the grouping of different perceived objects postulates Space. Perceptions of change farther constrain us to assume the condition of Time. The existence of living beings leads us to recognize a Soul; and the fact that some of these living beings are endowed with Reason, *i. e.* — have the faculty of bringing the Arts to the highest perfection, — necessitates our belief in a wise Creator, whose Reason has ordered everything for the best.

Notwithstanding the eternity of his five principles, Razi thus speaks of a Creator and even gives a story of Creation. First then a simple, pure, spiritual Light was created, the material of Souls, which are simple, spiritual substances, of the nature of Light. That Light-material or Upper-world, from which souls descended, is also called Reason, or Light of the Light of God. The Light is followed by the Shadow, from which the Animal Soul is created, for the service of the Rational Soul. But simultaneously with the simple, spiritual light, there existed from the first a composite form, which is Body, from the shadow of which now issue the four "natures", Warmth and Cold, Dryness and Moistness. From these four natures at last are formed all heavenly and earthly bodies. The whole process, however, is in operation from all eternity, without beginning in time, for God was never inactive.

That Razi was an astrologer is plain from his own utterances. The heavenly bodies consist indeed, according to him, of the same elements as earthly things, and the latter are continually exposed to the influences of the former.

6. Razi had to maintain a polemical attitude in two directions. On the one side he impugned the Muslim Unity of God, which could not bear to be associated with any eternal soul, matter, space or time; and on the other side he attacked the Dahrite system, which does not acknowledge any Creator of the world. This system, which is frequently mentioned by Muslim authors, with due aversion of course, appears to have found numerous representatives, though none of any importance. The adherents of the 'Dahr' (v. I, 2, § 2) are represented to us as Materialists, Sensualists, Atheists, Believers in the transmigration of souls, and so on; but we learn nothing more definite about their doctrines. In any case the Dahrites had no need to trace all that exists to a principle which was of spiritual essence and creative efficiency. Muslim Philosophy, on the other hand, did stand in need of such a principle, if it should only conform in some degree to the teaching of the faith. Natural Philosophy was not suited for the furtherance of this object, as it showed more interest in the manifold and often contrary operations of Nature than in the One Cause of all. Such aim was better attained by Neo-Platonic Aristotelianism, whose logico-metaphysical speculations endeavoured to trace all existence to one highest existence, or to derive all things from one supreme operative principle. But before we attend to this direction of thought, which commenced to appear even in the ninth century, we have still to give some account of an attempt to blend Natural Philosophy and the teachings of the Faith into a Philosophy of Religion.

2. THE FAITHFUL BRETHREN OF BASRA.

1. In the East, where every religion formed a State within the State, a political party invariably made its appearance in the additional character of a religious sect, just to gain adherents in some way or other. As a matter of principle indeed, Islam knew no distinction between men, — no caste or social standing. But property and education have the same influence everywhere; and in their train degrees of piety and stages of knowledge began to be set up, according as a community or party permitted of adjustment. Thus there arose secret societies having different grades, of which the highest and perhaps the next highest possessed an esoteric doctrine, which borrowed a good deal from the Natural Philosophy of the Neo-Pythagoreans. In furtherance of their object, which was to conquer political power, every expedient was regarded as lawful. For the initiated the Koran was explained allegorically. They traced their mystic lore, it is true, back to prophets with Biblical and Koranic names, but heathen philosophers were at the bottom of it all. Philosophy was completely transformed into a mythology of politics. The high intelligences and souls, which theoretic thinkers had recognized in the stars and planets, embodied themselves in human beings for the work of actual Politics; and it was declared to be a religious duty to assist these embodied intelligences in the establishment of an earthly kingdom of righteousness. The associations which acted in this way may best be compared to societies, which up to the days of Saint-Simonism and kindred phenomena in last century were wont to appear in countries where freedom of thought was restricted.

In the second half of the ninth century Abdallah ibn Maimun, head of the Karmatite party, was the originator of a movement of this kind. He was a Persian oculist, trained in the school of the Natural Philosophers. He proved able to associate both believers and freethinkers in a confederacy to endeavour to compass the overthrow of the Abbasid government. To the one set he was a conjurer, to the other a pious ascetic or learned philosopher. His colours were white, because his religion was that of the pure light, to which the soul was to ascend after its earthly wanderings. The duties inculcated were contempt for the body, disregard of the Material, community of goods for all the confederate brethren, as well as self-surrender to the confederacy, and fidelity and obedience to their chiefs, even to death, — for the society had its grades. In accordance with the sequence of existence, viz., God, Reason, Soul, Space and Time, they conceived the revelation of God to be made in history and in the constitution of their own brotherhood.

2. The chief homes of Karmatite activity were Basra and Kufa. Now we find in Basra in the second half of the tenth century a small association of men, whose confederacy aims at having four grades. We do not know, to be sure, how far the brethren succeeded in realizing the ideal organization of their confederacy. To the first grade belong young men of from 15 to 30 years of age, whose souls are being formed in the natural way: these must be completely submissive to their teachers. The second grade, — from 30 to 40 years of age — are introduced to secular wisdom, and receive an analogical knowledge of things. In the third grade, — from 40 to 50 years of

age — the Divine law of the world becomes known in more adequate form: that constitutes the stage of the prophets. Finally, in the highest grade, when one is over 50 years old, he comes to see the true reality of things, just like the blessed angels: he is exalted then above Nature, Doctrine and Law.

From this brotherhood there has come down to us a progressively-advancing Encyclopaedia of the Sciences of that day. It consists of 51 (originally perhaps 50) treatises, the contents of which are of such varied nature and origin that the redactors or compilers have not succeeded in establishing a complete harmony among them. In general, however, there is found in this Encyclopaedia an eclectic Gnosticism built on a foundation of Natural Science, and provided with a political background. The scheme sets out with mathematical considerations, continually playing with numbers and letters, and proceeds through Logic and Physics, — referring everything, however, to the Soul and its powers, — in order to approach at last, in a mystical and magical fashion, the knowledge of the Godhead. The whole representation is that of the doctrine of a persecuted sect, with the political features peeping out here and there. We see also something of suffering and struggle, — something of the oppressions to which the men of this Encyclopaedia or their predecessors were exposed, and something of the hope they cherished and the patience they preached. They seek in this spiritualistic philosophy, consolation or redemption: It is their religion. 'Faithful to death,' — so runs the expression — shall the brethren be, for to meet death for a friend's welfare, is the true Holy war. In life's pilgrimage through this world, —

thus the obligatory journey to Mecca is allegorized —, one must aid the other by all the means in his power. The rich must communicate to others a share of their material goods, and the wise a share of their intellectual possessions. But yet knowledge, as we have it in the Encyclopaedia, was probably reserved for initiated members of the highest grade.

It must be allowed, however, that this confraternity of the Faithful Brethren of Basra seems to have led a quiet existence, as perhaps was the case also with a branch-settlement of theirs in Bagdad. The relation of the Brethren to the Karmatites may have resembled that of the more peaceful Baptists to the revolutionary Anabaptists of the 'King of Sion'. [1]

The names of the following have been given to us by later writers, as having been members of the Brotherhood and collaborators of the Encyclopaedia, viz.: Abu Sulaiman Mohammed ibn Mushir al-Busti, called al-Muqaddasi; Abu-l-Hasan Ali ibn Harun al-Zandjani; Mohammed ibn Akhmed al-Nahradjuri; Al-Aufi and Zaid ibn Rifaa. In the time of their activity the Caliphate had already been forced to make an entire surrender of its secular power into the hands of the Shi'ite dynasty of the Buyids. Probably this circumstance was favourable to the appearance of an Encyclopaedia, in which Shi'ite and Mutazilite doctrines together with the results of Philosophy were comprehended in one popular system.

3. The Brethren themselves avow their eclecticism. They wish to collect the wisdom of all nations and religions. Noah and Abraham, Socrates and Plato, Zoroaster and

---

[1] [*Translator's note.* — 'John of Leyden']

Jesus, Mohammed and Ali are all prophets of theirs. Socrates, and Jesus and his apostles, no less than the children of Ali, are honoured as holy martyrs of their rational faith. The religious law in its literal sense is pronounced good for the ordinary man, — a medicine for weak and ailing souls: the deeper philosophic insight is for strong intelligences. Though the body is devoted to death, dying means rising again to the pure life of the Spirit, for those who during their earthly existence have been awakened by means of philosophic considerations out of careless slumber and foolish sleep. This is impressed with endless repetition, by means of legends and myths of later-Greek, Judaeo Christian, Persian or Indian origin. Every transitory thing is here turned into an emblem. On the ruins of positive religion and unsophisticated opinion a spiritualistic philosophy is built up, embracing all the knowledge and endeavour of human kind, so far as these came within the Brethren's field of view. The aim of their philosophizing is given as 'the assimilation of the soul to God, in the degree possible for man'.

In this scheme, the negative tendencies of the Brethren, are kept somewhat in the background, for reasons which are quite intelligible. But their criticism of human society and of positive religions is exhibited with least reserve in the 'Book of the Animal and the Man', in which the figurative dress makes it possible for them to represent animals as saying what might be questionable if heard from a human mouth.

4. The eclectic character of the scheme, and the far from systematic method adopted in its subdivisions render it difficult to give a coherent exposition of the philosophy

of the Brethren. But still the most important tenets, though sometimes loosely connected, must here be set forth with a measure of order.

The mental activity of Man falls to be divided, according to the Encyclopaedia, into Art and Science. Now Science or Knowledge is the form assumed within the knowing soul by that which is known, or a higher, finer, more intellectual mode of existence of whatever is realized in outward substance. Art on the other hand consists in projecting the form from the artist-soul into matter. Knowledge is potentially present in the soul of the disciple, but it becomes actual only through the teaching activity of a master, who carries knowledge as a reality within his own mind. But whence did it come to the first master? The Brethren answer, that according to the philosophers he gained it by his own reflection, while, according to the theologians, he received it through prophetic illumination; "but in our view there are various ways or instrumentalities by which knowledge may be attained. From the intermediate position of the soul, between the worlds of body and of mind it results that there are open to it three ways or sources of knowledge. Thus by means of the senses the soul is made acquainted with what is beneath it, and through logical inference with what is above it, and finally with itself by rational consideration or direct intuition. Of these kinds of knowledge the surest and the most deserving of preference is knowledge of one's self. When human knowledge attempts to go farther than this, it proves itself to be limited in many ways. Therefore one must not philosophize straight away about questions like the origin or the eternity of the world, but make his first essays with what is simpler. And only through renunciation of the world, and righteous conduct, does the soul lift itself gradually up to the pure knowledge of the Highest."

5. After secular instruction in Grammar, Poetry and History, and after religious education and doctrine, philosophic study should begin with the mathematical branches. Here everything is set forth in Neo-Pythagorean and Indian fashion. Not only numbers but even the letters of the alphabet are employed in childish trifling. It was particularly convenient for the Brethren that the number of letters in the Arabic alphabet is 28, or 4 multiplied by 7. Instead of proceeding according to practical and real points of view, they give the rein to fancy in all the sciences, in accordance with grammatical analogies and relations of numbers. Their Arithmetic does not investigate Number as such, but rather its significance. No search is made for any more suitable mode of expressing number in the case of phenomena; but things are themselves explained in accordance with the system of numbers. The Theory of number is Divine wisdom, and is above Things, for things are only formed after the pattern of numbers. The absolute principle of all existence and thought is the number One. The science of number, therefore, is found at the beginning, middle, and end of all philosophy. Geometry, with its figures addressing the eye, serves merely to make it more easily understood by beginners, but Arithmetic alone is true and pure science. And yet Geometry too is divided into a sensible form of it which deals with lines, surfaces and solids, and a pure or spiritual form which treats of the dimensions or properties of things, such as length, breadth and depth. The object both of Arithmetic and

Geometry is to conduct the soul from the sensible to the spiritual.

First of all then they lead us to consider the stars. Now the Encylopaedia offers us, in its Astrology, — and nothing else could be expected — teaching which is exceedingly fantastic and sometimes self-contradictory. The whole of it is pervaded by the conviction that the stars not merely foretell the future, but directly influence or bring about every thing that happens beneath the moon. Fortune and misfortune come equally from them. Jupiter, Venus and the Sun bring fortune; misfortune is brought, on the other hand, by Saturn, Mars and the Moon; while the effects produced by the planet Mercury have in them both bad and good. Mercury is the lord of education and science: we owe to him our knowledge, which comprises bad and good. In the same way too the other planets have all their several spheres of influence; and man in the course of life, if he is not prematurely snatched away, experiences successively the influences of the whole of the heavenly bodies. The Moon causes his body to grow and Mercury forms his mind. Then he comes under the sway of Venus. The Sun gives him family, riches or dominion; Mars, bravery and noble-mindedness. Thereupon, under the guidance of Jupiter, he prepares, by means of religious exercises, for the journey to the world beyond, and he attains rest under the influence of Saturn. Many men, however, do not live long enough, or are not enabled by circumstances, to develope their natural capacities in unbroken sequence. God therefore graciously sends them his prophets, by whose teaching they may, even in a short time and under unfavourable circumstances, form their natures completely.

6. According to the Encyclopaedia, Logic is related to
Mathematics. In fact just as Mathematics conducts from
the sensible to the intellectual, so Logic takes an intermediate position. between Physics and Metaphics. In Physics
we have to do with bodies; in Metaphysics, with pure
Spirits; but Logic treats of the ideas of the latter as well
as of the representations of the former in our soul. Yet
in range and importance Logic is inferior to Mathematics.
For the subject of Mathematics is regarded not merely as
an intermediary, but also as the essence of the All, while
on the other hand Logic remains completely restricted to
psychic forms as an intermediary between body and mind.
Things are regulated by numbers, but our presentations
and ideas by things.

The logical observations of the Brethren start from Porphyry's Introduction, and the Categories, the Hermeneutics
and the Analytics of Aristotle. They present nothing original, or very little.

To the five terms of Porphyry, a sixth, — the 'Individual' — is added, no doubt for the sake of symmetry.
Three of these, — Genus, Species, Individual, — are then
called Objective Qualifications and three, — Difference,
Property, Accident — Abstract or Conceptional Qualifications. The Categories are Genus-conceptions, of which the
first is Substance, the other nine denoting its Accidents.
The whole system of Concepts is farther developed by a
division into species. But besides Division, there are three
additional logical methods in use: Analysis, Definition and
Deduction. Analysis is the method for beginners, because
it permits a knowledge of what is individual. More subtle,
however, as disclosing to us what is spiritual, — are

Definition and Deduction, the former investigating the
essential nature of Species, and the latter that of Genera.
The Senses apprise us of the existence of things; but ac-
quaintance with the essence of things is gained by reflection.
The information which is conveyed to us by the senses
is small, as it were the letters of the alphabet. Of greater
importance considerably are the principles of rational
knowledge, just as words have more significance than
letters; but the most important knowledge of all, lies in
the propositions which have been derived from those principles, and which the human mind gains for itself or ap-
propriates, in contradistinction to that knowledge which
Nature or the Divine revelation has imparted to it.

7. From God, the highest Being, who is exalted above
all distinctions and oppositions both of the Material and
the Spiritual, the whole world is derived by the path of
Emanation. If now and again a Creation is spoken of,
that is only to be understood as a form of adaptation to
theological language. The gradation then of the Emanations
is exhibited as follows: 1. The Creative Spirit. ($\nu o \tilde{u} \varsigma$, 'aql);
2. The Passive Spirit, or the All-Soul or World-Soul; 3. The
First Material; 4. The Operative Nature, a power of the
World-Soul; 5. The Absolute Body, called also, the Second
Material; 6. The World of the Spheres; 7. The Elements of
the Sublunary World; 8. The Minerals, Plants and Animals
composed of these elements. These then are the eight
Essences which, — together with God, the Absolute One,
who is in everything and with everything — complete the
series of Original Essences corresponding to the nine Car-
dinal Numbers.

Spirit, Soul, Original Matter, and Nature are simple;

but with Body we enter the realm of the Composite. Here all is composed of Matter and Form, or, — to adopt another principle of division, — of Substance and Accident. The first Substances are Matter and Form; the first Accidents or Properties, Space, Motion and Time, to which in the opinion of the Brethren may perhaps be added Tone and Light. Matter is one; all plurality and diversity come from the Forms. Substance is designated also as the constitutive, material Form, while Accident is the completing, spiritual Form. The Encyclopaedia does not express itself clearly on these points. But in any case Substantiality is looked for rather in the Universal than in the Particular, and Form is put before Matter. The Substantial Form, like a spectre, frightens off every attempt of the philosopher to investigate thoroughly the domain of the Material. The Forms wander at their own sweet will like lords through the lower world of Matter. No trace is discoverable of any inner relation between Matter and Form. Not only in thought, but also in reality they keep themselves separate.

From the account which has been given an idea may now be formed of the story of Nature as the Brethren viewed it. They have been represented as the Darwinists of the tenth century, but nothing could be more inappropriate. The various realms of Nature, it is true, yield according to the Encyclopaedia an ascending and connected series; but the relation is determined not by bodily structure, but by the inner Form or Soul-Substance. The Form wanders in mystic fashion from the lower to the higher and *vice versa*, not in accordance with inner laws of formation, or modified to suit external conditions, but in accordance with the influences of the stars, and, in the case of Man at least, in accordance with practical and theoretical behaviour. To give a history of Evolution in the modern sense of the term was very far from the thought of the Brethren. For example they expressly insist that the horse and the elephant resemble Man more than the ape does, although the bodily likeness is greater in the last-named. In fact in their system the body is a matter of quite secondary consideration: the death of the body is called the birth of the soul. The soul alone is an efficient existence, which procures the body for itself.

8. The teaching of the Brethren concerning Nature is therefore merged almost completely in Psychology. Let us confine ourselves here to the human soul. It stands in the centre of the All; and just as the World is a huge man, Man is a little world.

The human soul has emanated from the World-soul; and the souls of all individuals taken together constitute a substance which might be denominated the Absolute Man or the Spirit of Humanity. Every individual soul, however, is involved in Matter, and must gradually be formed into spirit. To that end it possesses many faculties or powers, and of these the speculative faculties are the choicest, for knowledge is the very life of the soul.

The soul of the child is at first like a white sheet of paper. What the five senses convey to it is first presented, then judged, and lastly stored up, in the front, middle, and hinder parts of the brain respectively. Through the faculty of speech and the art of writing, which make up the number of the internal senses to five, corresponding to the number of the External, the contents of Presentation are then realized.

Among the external senses, Hearing takes precedence of Sight; for Sight, a mere slave of the moment, is occupied with what is actually present to the sense, whereas Hearing apprehends also what is past, and is conscious of the harmony of the tuneful spheres. Hearing and Sight constitute the group of the intellectual senses, whose effect must continue time without end.

While Man then possesses the external senses in common with the lower animals, the specific nature of human reason is notified in Judgment, Speech and Action. Reason judges of good and bad, and in conformity with that judgment the will is determined. But in particular the significance which Language has for the soul's life of cognition is to be emphasised. A concept which cannot be denoted by some expression in some language is not thinkable at all. The word is the body of the thought, which cannot exist absolutely *per se*.

But it is difficult to see how this understanding of the relation between concept and expression is to square with other opinions of the Brethren.

9. At its highest stage the teaching of the Brethren becomes a Philosophy of Religion. Its purpose is a reconciliation between Science and Life, Philosophy and Faith. Now in these matters men differ greatly. The ordinary man requires a sensuous worship of God; but just as the souls of animals and plants are beneath the soul of the ordinary man, so above it are the souls of the philosopher and the prophet with whom the pure angel is associated. In the higher stages the soul is raised also above the lower popular religion with its sensuous conceptions and usages.

No doubt Christianity and the Zoroastrian faith appeared

to the Brethren to be more perfect religious revelations. 'Our Prophet, Mohammed', they said, 'was sent to an uncivilized people, composed of dwellers in the desert, who neither possessed a proper conception of the beauty of this world, nor of the spiritual character of the world beyond. The crude expressions of the Koran, which are adapted to the understanding of that people, must be understood in a spiritual sense by those who are more cultured'.

But the truth is not presented in its purity even in the other national religions. There is a rational faith above them all for which the Brethren moreover tried to find a metaphysical derivation. Between God and his first creature, the Creative Spirit, there is interposed by way of hypostasis the Divine World-Law (nâmûs). That World-Law extends over everything, and is the wise arrangement of a merciful Creator, who intends evil |to no one. Belief in a God of Anger, in the punishment of Hell and the like, the Brethren declare to be irrational. Such a faith does harm to the soul. The ignorant, sinful soul finds its hell even in this life and in its own body. On the other hand, Resurrection is the separation of the soul from its body, and the great Resurrection at the last day is the separation of the Universal soul from the world, and its return to God. This turning to God indeed is the aim in all religions.

10. The ethical system of the Brethren has an ascetic, spiritualistic character, although here too their eclecticism is shewn. According to it man is acting rightly, when he follows his proper nature; 'praiseworthy is the free act of the soul; admirable are the actions which have proceeded from rational consideration; and lastly, obedience to the Divine World-Law is worthy of the reward of being raised

to the celestial world of spheres. But this requires longing
for what is above; and therefore the highest virtue is Love,
which strives after union with God, the first loved one,
and which is evinced even in this life in the form of
religious patience and forbearance with all created beings.
Such love gains in this life serenity of soul, freedom of
heart and peace with the whole world, and in the life to
come ascension to Eternal Light.'

After all this we need not wonder that the body was
depreciated a good deal. 'Our true essence is the soul, and
the highest aim of our existence should be to live, with
Socrates, devoted to the Intellect, and with Christ, to the
Law of Love. Nevertheless the body must be properly
treated and looked after in order that the soul may have
time to attain its full development.' In this view the
Brethren set up an ideal type of human culture, whereof
the features were borrowed from the characteristics of various
nations. 'The ideal, and morally perfect man, should be
of East-Persian derivation, Arabic in faith, of Irak, i. e.
Babylonian, education, a Hebrew in astuteness, a disciple
of Christ in conduct, as pious as a Syrian Monk, a Greek
in the individual sciences, an Indian in the interpretation
of all mysteries, but lastly and especially, a Sufi in his
whole spiritual life.'

11. The attempt to establish in this way a reconciliation
between knowledge and faith satisfied neither side.
Theological dialecticians looked down upon the interpretation of the Koran given by the Brethren, just as the
divines of our day look down upon the N. T. exegesis of
Count Tolstoi. And the more rigid Aristotelians regarded
the Pythagorean-Platonic tendency of the Encyclopaedia

much as a modern professor of philosophy is wont to look upon Spiritism, Occultism, and phenomena of that nature. But the writings, or at any rate the opinions, of the Faithful Brethren of Basra have exercised an important influence on the great body of the educated or half-educated world, — an influence to which eloquent attestation is borne by the very fact that so many manuscripts, mostly of recent date, are to be met with, of this extensive Encyclopaedia. Among many sects within the world of Islam, such as the Batinites, the Ismaelites, the Assasins, the Druses, or whatever may be their names, we find again the same doctrines in the main. In this form Greek wisdom has best succeeded in making itself at home in the East, while the Aristotelian School-Philosophy would only thrive, with few exceptions, in the hothouse-cultivation bestowed upon it at the courts of princely patrons. The great religious father, Gazali, is ready enough to toss aside the wisdom of the Brethren as mere popular philosophy, but he does not hesitate to take over what was good in them. He owes more to their body of ideas than he would perhaps have cared to avow. And their treatises have been turned to profit by others besides, particularly in Encyclopaediac works. The influence of the Encyclopaedia continues even yet in the Muslim East. In vain was it burned in Bagdad in the year 1150, along with the writings of Ibn Sina.

This is the end of this publication.

Any remaining blank pages are for our book binding requirements and are blank on purpose.

To search thousands of interesting publications like this one, please remember to visit our website at:

http://www.kessinger.net

LaVergne, TN USA
23 December 2009

168014LV00001B/11/A

9 781425 367947